Conversations
with the Night

A POETIC MEMOIR

ANDRES FERNANDEZ

I

Conversations with the Night

Cover Art by Kat Savage of Savage Hart Book Services
Edited by Nicole Wong & Alicia Cook

ISBN-13: 978-0-692-77944-6
ISBN-10: 0-692-77944-2

Thank You.

To everyone that has endured me through the process of my becoming.

Huge thanks to both Jacqueline Bird and Alicia Cook for helping me review the final draft.

To Kat Savage for handling the formatting and cover of this book.

To my good friend and private client who gave me the time freedom I needed to finish this book.

To my healer and good friend, Martin (Marty) Marquez.

To my mother for always believing in me.

To my children for showing me what love is.

And lastly, to every single one of you who have supported me throughout my writing journey.

Right and Wrong
Los Angeles, 2015

Within the first few years of our domestication,
life instills us with dogmas of right and wrong.

Beliefs and life lessons
are handed down like heirlooms.

I never fell for religion;
so many revolve around fear.

Yet there is one belief that seeped fully
into to my core,
making it nearly impossible
to find peace with my decisions—

"When you have kids, you are to marry."

1992

Freewill

City Terrace, 1992

Mother orders us to stay inside
while she takes a shower.

As soon as the restroom door shuts
and we hear the lock turn,
Junior, Walter, and I run outside,
knowing we only have twenty minutes to play.

Walter is the middle child, two years older than I,
and Junior is the eldest, two years older than Walter.

"Stay down here! Me and Walter are gonna pull you up
from the top with the broom!"
Junior squeals, as they make their way to the top of the
six-foot cliff.

As he says, they do.

"Climb down, Walter. It's your turn.
We're gonna pull you up now!"

As he says, we do.

"It's my turn," he runs down.
"You guys pull me up on the count of three, okay?
One, two, three!"

We pull and pull, but not even our best is enough.
He was half way up when our strength gives out.

"I'm gonna let go!" Junior screams.

As he says, he does.

"You guys fucken suck,"
Junior gets upset.

I frown because it strikes as truth.

"Junior, your hand is bleeding!" Walter cries.

It only takes a second
before he sees the stream of blood
running down his fingers and
dripping onto the floor.

Junior runs inside, face pale, palm up,
and calling for Mother like a little girl.

Bewildered by what just happened,
I look around for the cause and find
a layer of my brother's flesh hanging to dry
from the old clothesline pole
with rusty jagged edges.

Fifteen minutes.
Fifteen minutes is all we need
to rush Junior to the E.R
for twenty-seven stitches
beginning at his wrist and
ending at the bottom of his ring finger.
We never do listen to
Mother's good intentions,
all we ever hear is a nagging woman.

Right Hook

East Los Angeles, 1992

The smell of tequila slaps me in the face
as my father brags about me.

"This is my little Julio Cesar Chavez!"
he tells the man with the belly
that hangs over the fly of his pants.
I'm picturing the man's fat fingers
making a napkin of his white
salsa-smeared button-up.

"That kid is too small to be a fighter!
Come on, show me what you've got!"
the filthy man slurs through drunk lips
as he taps his flabby cheeks.

I glance at my father for approval.
He takes a sip from his tequila,
makes a fist, taps the left side of his chin,
and points at the man.

"As hard as you can, Mijo!"
he gives me the green light.

The fat man's smile wears mockery
and some salt from the tortilla chips.

With a clenched fist and a nice wind-up,
I release the heaviest right hook
possible from a four-year-old.

"What happened?"

my father yells at the man through laughter
while parading me around.

"The tooth was already loose, cabron!"
the man garbles with his shirt in his mouth.

On the bright side, it was no longer so obvious
his shirt was stained with salsa.
It all just looks like blood and drool.

Halloween
City Terrace, 1992

We arrive home from a long night of
trick-or-treating.

We must have walked at least five miles.
Our faces don paint that has cracked and
almost smeared away with the sweat.

Because of rumors she heard on the television,
Mother inspects the candy
for poison, razors,
and needles.

She grants us each three pieces before bedtime.

The front door swings open,
and through it my drunken father toddles.
I run toward him for a hug.

"Don't be so needy," he pulls me off his leg,
discarding me like sketchy candy.

"Why are they eating so much candy?
Don't you know it rots their fucken teeth?!"
he belittles Mother, teeth holding a cigarette.

"They don't eat candy every day,"
our mother pleads,
"I put the rest away."

"You want them to lose their fucken teeth?!"
he continues while storming into the kitchen,

toward the bags of candy,
"Don't be so fucken stupid!"

Grabbing the bags and tying them into knots,
he walks out the front door and flings them across the
grassy slope.

We cry.
Mother tries to calm us down.
Father falls onto the couch and sleeps peacefully.

Grudges
City Terrace, 1992

The mice bite through the cereal boxes and
the bags of rice
we keep on the high shelf of the cupboard.

So Father buys traps to get rid of them.

The first trapped mouse lives,
but it couldn't escape the adhesive trap on which it finds
itself.

My drunken father laughs at the rodent's helplessness.

He pinches its tail
with his thumb and index finger
then yanks the squealing mouse
off the trap to bring it outside.

With one quick spin, it bites his finger.
He curses it as he drops it onto the floor.
Father tries to stomp it with his boots
and watches it run into the shrubs
in front of our home.

I never saw adhesive traps again.

He makes sure to buy the ones that snap necks
and make the little critters shit themselves.

Follow the Leader
City Terrace to Fontana, 1992

Cars, couches, dining table,
television, radio, beds, and dressers—
loaded onto a flatbed.
Cups, bowls, plates, blender, pots and pans—
wrapped in newspaper, packed in boxes,
and sealed shut with a single strip of duct tape.
Clothes, VHS movies, toys, towels, and blankets—
stuffed in heavy duty trash bags.

Father needs distance from the life he created.
Mother follows him to Hell and back
like a "good woman" should.
My brothers and I are dragged along for the ride.

A new home awaits us out in the middle of nowhere.
I hope it doesn't have mice or booze.

Making Mud
Fontana, 1992

Fiery enough to force bare feet into dance,
the heat rises from the ground.

Junior points the hose towards the sky.
The water reaches to put out the sun.

Drops thump onto the red dirt,
quenching its thirst,
and the earth releases the scent of relief.

We laugh cheerfully,
scream joyously,
and run around in circles,
making mud and memories.

The Snake

Fontana, 1992

Junior is the most helpful of us brothers.
He feeds the chickens, while Walter and I sit
in Father's Porsche and Bug, pretending to race.
We bask in the balminess of the day.

"Hey! You guys!"
my father screams
as he walks toward us
from the grassy lot behind our home.
In his hand is a dead snake longer than I am tall.

"You see? This is why I tell you guys
not to go back there,"
he gestures sternly at the carcass.

I ask if we'll bury it.
Junior asks if we could make it into a belt for him.
Walter caresses its cold, scaly body.
"Why are you afraid?" he asks me, "It's dead."

I do not fear the snake.
It is the blood on my father's hands
that makes me uneasy.

Raising Men
Fontana, 1992

While Mother cleans the kitchen,
I wake from a nap.

My father and brothers are
out back working on the cars.

"Mom, do you need help?" I ask.

"Of course, Mijo. Help me sweep the floor,"
she points toward a broom.

I pick it up and swirl dust around for a few minutes
before my father appears.

"Don't you turn my boys into maricones!"
his voice thunders through the kitchen.
"Men don't sweep!
Take that broom away before I do!"
With that, he storms away
without a second glance at me.

Mother kneels down and kisses my forehead,
"You didn't do anything wrong.
Go call your brothers in. It's getting dark."

Se los va llevar el Diablo

Fontana, 1992

For my brothers and me,
sleep was almost impossible—
three boys with overactive imaginations
crammed into a room.

Giggles and guffaws leak through thin walls
and under the door,
drawing Mother into the room.

Eyes half shut and hair a mess,
she hisses at us,
"Se los va llevar el diablo si no se van a dormir!"

(The devil is gonna come get you if you don't go to sleep!)

I was never sure if they fell asleep
or if, like me, fear sealed their lips
as we waited to be dragged to Hell.

Caldo de Pollo

Fontana, 1992

Mother prepared caldo de pollo,
with carrots, cabbage, chayote, potato,
and a fresh chicken from the coop.

She serves me, and I ask her to remove the chicken claw
from my bowl.

"That's the best part,"
my father says as he reaches over,
grabs the claw from my plate,
and begins sucking on it.
"It has the most flavor," he continues.

I eat the veggies and even ask for more.
I try the chicken, but don't like the texture
or the bones that I have to extract.
The warm soup is my favorite.

"I noticed that you don't like chicken,"
Mother glances at all the chicken left in my bowl
and then at me.

Father gives her a glare of disapproval
then gives the same one to me.

"Meat is protein. Makes you stronger.
Feeds your muscles. You need meat, Mijo.
You want to be strong; like a real man,"
he flexes his bicep,
"You're not getting up 'till you eat all your chicken."

All I could do is sit there
as everyone finishes their soup
and leaves the table one by one.

Cleaning the table,
Mother takes my bowl
while my father looks away.

My mother is soft and understanding.
My father, stoic and set in his ways.
I am only a child, acquiring taste.

Good Mornings
Fontana, 1992

I run to the restroom to dry my clothes
in front of the wall-mounted heater.
My brothers are there already.

"Hurry, before father wakes!"
I hear their strained whispers
as they run back to the room.

Two minutes later,
Father walks in and finds me.

"Again?! How many times do I have to tell you before
you listen?!"
he opens the shower door
and turns the knob to freezing cold, "Get in!"

As the soles of work boots pound
against the bathroom tiles on his way out,
I hurry to remove my half wet clothes
knowing he'd return shortly.

I jump in. The bathroom door creaks.
The shower door opens
as cold water stabs at my back.
The pain flees as I see what is coming.

"This is the only way you'll learn,"
his belt's leather smacks against my wet skin.

I wet the bed till I was twelve-years-old.
These days my mother blames trauma.

Those days my father blamed ignorance.

Becoming
Fontana, 1992

Black teardrops swim in the stagnant water ducts
in front of our home.

We scoop one up with a KFC Styrofoam cup
we found on the side of the road
and pour it into the plastic tank
where our turtle once lived.

"It's gonna turn into a frog, guys.
My teacher told me," Junior jumps up and down.

Every day after school, we examine the little tadpole.

The hind legs push their way out of the slimy skin.
Two weeks later, the forelimbs follow.
Then, the head morphs into itself.
The little creature grows out of its tail,
and we finally have a pet frog
just like Junior said we would.

Releasing it daily onto the blacktop of our driveway,
we watch it hop around
and try to catch it all over again.

It only lives for three days
before Walter accidently steps on it.

Life is strange,
it takes so long to become
and can end so fast.

The Sound of Escaping Hope
Fontana, 1992

Screams rattle the walls harder than
the slam of the door
when Father gets home that night.

We run through the kitchen door,
finding Mother and dinner
scattered across the floor;
tranquility taken by brutal force.

The self-righteous drunk with hell in his eyes
raises his hand one last time.

My brothers scurry and stand between them
with arms high, creating a wall,
as I hold Mother in my tiny arms.

"Leave her alone! Leave! Just leave!"
they command as loud as their lungs allow.

"You raised a bunch of maricones," he slurs
as he storms out of the back door.

Mother sends us away,
cleans up the mess on the floor,
puts away the mess in her head,
then cooks for us, feeds us, bathes us,
and lays us in bed to rest.

She is an angel for wanting us to have a father
the way she never did.
He is a demon who lied his way into her heart.

Gentle shakes from Mother wake us one by one
in the middle of the night,
"Come on, boys. We're going to the store."

She wraps me in a blanket and carries me to the car,
asking my brothers to follow.

My father, in the passenger seat,
smiles at us and says,
"We're gonna come right back, boys.
Your mom is just taking me to the gas station
for beer because I can't drive anymore."

My father rides with the window down,
smoking cigarette after cigarette,
and I notice the moon following me with every turn.
We pull up into a gas station, and he tells
my mother to park next to the air pump.

"I'll be right back. I'm just going to run inside,"
he steps out.

He must have felt it in his cold bones, in his chest,
that rush of fear
that stands up every hair behind your neck,
that cold sweat that warns you
when something disturbing is about to happen.

Slamming the door, he lights another cigarette,
leans in through the window, turns off the ignition,
and takes the keys,
"Do you think I'm fucken stupid?"
he laughs in my mother's face.

Every muscle in her neck surrenders,
her head falls onto the steering wheel,
and her tears fall onto her lap.
Father circles the car,
deflating tires.
Through the hiss,
I can hear the sound of escaping hope.

1993

Something Missing

Fontana, 1993

"Is everyone here?"
the photographer at Food 4 Less
asks my mother
while he sets up the background
for our photo.

"Y-yes,"
the angel replies hesitantly.
"Come on, boys."

The appointment had been set
months prior to the day.
Our button-ups and pants hung
ironed for several weeks.
Mother even bought a nice dress for the occasion.

We pose in front of the midnight-hued backdrop,
and Mother tries her best not to blend in with it.

"Okay, on the count of three, I need everyone to smile!
One...two...three!"

The flash goes off.

"Two more! One...two...three!"

The flash goes off.

"One more, without Mom!"

She walks out of the shot.

"One...two...three!"

The flash goes off.

Our smiles are genuine;
but Mother only smiles on cue.

This is our first family portrait,
and something is missing
other than Mother's mind.

Filthy City Streets
Downtown Los Angeles, 1993

Sitting in the backseat of the car
in front of the Los Angeles Courthouse,
I gaze out the window
at all the trash overflowing from bins,
the people smoking cigarettes
and tossing butts into drains,
the homeless asking for change
and sleeping on cardboard beds,
crowds waiting for their bus around a single bench,
construction workers breaking cement.
Silence didn't exist in a place like this.

You could hear the waves of cars on the highway,
the honking of horns from cars leaving driveways,
the roar of buses pulling in and out of stops,
the police sirens howling in the distance.
Thousands of voices muffled by noise pollution.

I spot my mother walking toward the car.
She looks at me, smiles, then chases her breath
and loses her balance as the man passing on a bicycle
yanks off her gold chain
with the Virgin Mary medallion.

Running to the car, she checks her window reflection for
scrapes on her neck.
I can see the pain filling her eyes.

She doesn't care for the gold,
her tears are rooted much deeper
than the loss of precious metal.

That necklace was the only thing she had left
that belonged to her mother,
my grandmother, and my godmother,
and she lost it to the mess of these filthy city streets.

Kissing Glass
Wayside Correctional Facility, 1993

Maze-like lines fill with women and children.
Speakers call the next in line
to numbered windows with aggravated clerks.

Sometimes we'd be there
for two or three hours,
basking in all sorts of smoke
before gaining entry.

The speaker, distorted and muffled,
calls my mother's name.

We walk to the tall counter
and a guard, too big for the chair he sits on,
escorts us into the next room.

There is a phone hinged on the wall
in front of a three-by-three window
lined with what looks like chicken wire
and a single chair for us to sit in.
Mother's request for a second chair is denied.

Moments later, Father walks up
to the window in his orange jumpsuit.
The officer removes his cuffs and says,
"You have twenty minutes."

Father smiles at us.
I smile back.
Mother picks up the phone and cries,
"This is so hard on me…"

They talk forever
as I play with chewed gum
stuck beneath the counter.

Finally, I get to talk.
I don't know what to say or how to behave.
I don't understand the concept of jail yet.

But I notice he treats us a lot nicer
in here than he does at home.

He'll say,
"How are you?"
and "I love you, Mijo."

...you know,
all those things a kid should be used to hearing.

"Two more minutes,"
the guard says as he taps my father's shoulder.
His smile dulls,
and he presses his hand against the glass.

Mother sets hers directly over his
as the tears flow through river beds
then fall onto her lips.
He places his other hand on the glass,
smiles at me with sad eyes,
"Tell your brothers I love them
and miss them.
Take care of your mom."

Mother always told me
to give him a kiss goodbye,

but I never did.

I only ever kissed the glass between us.

New Friends
Fontana, Boyle Heights, City Terrace, 1993

Excitement gleaming in my eyes
and a new backpack filled with new supplies,
I hold my mother's hand as she walks me
into my first kindergarten classroom.

The teachers and kids speak English.
I stutter with every response,
anxious because of my broken tongue.

My only friend is a little boy
whose name I cannot remember.
He carries a Batman lunchbox
and always shares his Lunchable with me
...even the chocolate.
I never get to say goodbye to him.
We abruptly move back to the City
when my father lands in prison,
and I have to move schools
three weeks into my first school year.

Confusion seeping from my mind
and a head full of questions I will not dare ask,
I hold my mother's hand as she walks me
into my second kindergarten class.

The teachers and kids speak English and Spanish.
I whisper every response,
unsure if I should speak up.

My only friends are two little girls
whose names I cannot remember.

They are inseparable
and always give me their fruit cups
... even the ones in gelatin.
I never get to say goodbye to them.
We move closer to my aunt's
when my mother gets a second job,
and I have to move schools
three months into my first school year.

Disconnection in my eyes
and a heart filled with answers I don't want to carry,
I get dropped off at school by Mother
before she drives to work,
and Walter walks me to my third Kindergarten class.

The teachers and kids speak English and Spanish,
I bite my tongue
and don't waste time making friends.

1994

The Earth Rattles
Boyle Heights, 1994

The earth rattles mercilessly,
filling the City with fear,
but it does not shake me from my slumber.
What wakes me is Mother's screams
as she guides my brothers out of the house
through falling dishes, picture frames,
and light fixtures.

Looking around the room,
I find empty beds,
blankets falling off from them,
broken glass, and a blue light
coloring the once-white walls.
As my bare feet touch the cold floor,
the shaking stops,
and I can hear Mother
tell my brothers to wait outside
as she runs in to get me.

They cry but obey.

When she picks me up
the earth rattles again.
We make our way towards the door,
and I can see her crystal glassware
crashing onto the hard tile
before the whole shelf comes down behind us.

My brothers run to us
and greet us with a giant hug
as we exit the front door.

The whole neighborhood is outside
with blankets, flashlights, and lit candles.
The older women,
with rosaries wrapped around their hands,
recite prayers for the rest of the shivering city.

I watch them quietly
as tears of fear fall from their eyes,
and I can almost see their hearts
light up with concern.

It is a tragically beautiful sight
to witness them love those they do not know.

Rock-Throwing Contest
Buelah, 1994

My older cousin picks up a quarter-sized rock,
runs his fingers through its coarseness for a few seconds,
then challenges,
"Let's see who can throw the furthest."

The kid has a slingshot for an arm
that few could match.
He's one of the best pitchers in our family.

One by one, we pick up pebbles
—some small, some large,
some made of dirt, and some made of rock—
and throw them across the empty lot.

Walter and my cousin
out throw each other with every fling.
I don't stand a chance, and Junior's arm gives out,
but we stay to watch.

One stone hits the carport
from the house down below,
then the next one breaks a flowerpot,
and finally, one flies through a kitchen window.

We celebrate for a second, then declare our cousin the
winner and run inside.

Ten minutes pass before a daunting knock
rattles our door.
Mother walks out of the restroom in her towel
to find an upset older woman.

44

"Your stupid children broke my kitchen window!"
the woman points.

"Excuse me?!" Mother replies,
"Those are my kids you're talking about!"

"I saw them run inside after they did it.
You're going to pay for my window!"

"I'm not paying for shit," Mother fights back.
"My boys have been inside watching cartoons all day."

The adamant woman does not budge,
so Mother curses her out and tells her to fuck off while
slamming the door.

An eerie stillness fills the room
when Mother turns to find us all
staring at her while Maury plays
in the background,
talking about a woman with a peach phobia.
We smile at her,
but it doesn't mean a thing.
Mother's face clearly says "run"
as she disconnects the iron and exclaims,
"Van a ver cabrones!"

Macaroni & Cheese

City Terrace, 1994

Mother works well into the afternoon,
so my aunt who lives upstairs
invites us for dinner every once in a while.

My aunt loves drinking, and the relationship
she has with my uncle is entertaining.
He makes jokes at everything, and she screams a lot.
He can kill a twelve pack of Cokes.
She can kill a twelve pack of Miller Lite.
They love each other, I think.

She sits us at the round table in her small kitchen
and drops a spooned glop of macaroni and cheese onto
each plate
next to the carne asada and pile of beans.

She sits a can of Coke in front of each of us
at arm's length
and tells us we can't have it
until we finish all of our food.

I eat the beans that are amazing as always,
try the macaroni but don't like it,
and give Junior the carne asada.

Noticing my macaroni isn't going anywhere
she reminds me sternly that I can't have the soda
until I finish my entire meal.

I don't want to tell her that I don't like it.
I'm afraid she might yell at me.

She's a small woman, but she's fierce.
She scares the shit out of me with a single glance and
flare of her nostrils.

"Okay. Can I have some water instead?"

"You should be grateful that you have food on your
plate! Growing up, we didn't have someone to cook for
us!" her hands begin to tremble.
"You're not getting up from that chair
until you finish!"

I fall asleep on the chair that afternoon,
and no one wakes me until Mother gets home.

"Your father used to do that when you were smaller. Do
you remember that?"
Mother asks as she carries me downstairs.

"Yes," I reply, "Why are they always so mean?"

"They're not mean," she answers.
"They just never learned how to show love."

1995

Bombing

City Terrace, 1995

Two fishtail skateboards, nine kids,
and one hill running for three hundred feet
before splitting at a fork—
to the left side, a straightaway,
and to the right side,
a forty-five-degree hill.

Being one of the youngest in the crew,
I always feel the need to prove myself.
So, I sit on the fishtail
with my feet still on the ground
and glance at the cousin sitting on the other board.

"Just pick up your legs when you're ready.
The hill will pull you down. Just don't shit yourself."
he says, lifting both feet,
sending himself down the hill
while laughing exuberantly.

With a deep breath and a tight grip on the board,
I lift my feet off the floor and set them on the nose.

Nothing happens.
I look around and under the board.
There's a tiny pebble under the wheel.

It makes me think twice.
Maybe I'm not supposed to do this;
but before the second thought finishes,
a pair of hands give me a forceful push from behind,
and I am off.

The wheels gripping asphalt sound like jet engines.
The sweat on my palms
dries with momentum's gust.
I lean right and feel weightless
as my small body reaches the horizon.

The front wheels dive into the monstrous hill.
My breath—now two seconds behind me—
is harder to keep steady
than the speed wobbles that shake me uncontrollably.

Finally, I reach a stop at the top of a small hill
where my cousin stands waiting for me, laughing.

The dread wipes all color clean off my face,
and my hands can't stop shaking.

"Get up. I need to check your pants,"
he smirks, and we both explode into laughter.

Dirt Wars
City Terrace, 1995

The rules are simple:
No crying.
Dirt clods only.
No throwing hard.

Ten minutes into the war,
someone always breaks the third rule,
the victim breaks the first,
and vengeance breaks the second.

Freeze Tag
City Terrace, 1995

We're deciding who will be 'it'
for our game of freeze tag.
The process of elimination narrows it to the last two.

"Bubble gum, bubble gum in a dish,
how many pieces do you wish?"
the good girl asks.

"Two!" I grin,
knowing this would free me.

"One, two..."
silence lingers as her finger hovers over my foot,
"...and you will not be it
for the rest of your entire life.
I'm out! You're it!" she jumps for joy.

My face turns red, my fists clench,
"You fucken cheated!
I said two, and you made up some stupid shit
so you wouldn't be 'it'!"

She knows nobody will believe me.
I have a bad rep for a short temper.

"It's the new way of doing it;
if you're gonna be a cry baby,
you're not gonna play."

I march over to the lemon tree crawling with ants,
rest my head on the dusty bark, close my eyes,

and counts to fifty as the rest of my siblings disperse.

I understand the bed I made
and hate lying in it.
I also understand my frustration.

There are about sixteen kids
to freeze on a two-acre lot.
This game is rigged;
the good kids are never 'it'.

Tangerine Summers
City Terrace, 1995

"We're gonna give you a boost.
Get as many as you can,"
Junior says, handing
me a plastic grocery bag.

The branches are too feeble
to carry even their own weight,
but I don't complain.

I like helping,
but I am small and often too weak.

By the count of three, I'm on the first branch,
maneuvering my limbs through those of the tree.

"Get that big one!" says Junior.

"That one too!" follows Walter.

Ants crawl all over my skin.
They tickle until I feel the first pinch.
I fight the pain until one makes it under my shorts,
biting me right on the nuts.

I drop the bag immediately and jump off the tree,
tearing my uniform and scraping my neck
on a branch on the way down.

"What happened!?" Junior eyes widen.

"An ant bit me in the balls!"

"Damn, you got bit in the balls,
and Mom is gonna kick your ass when she gets home for
ripping your shirt!"

Thunderous laughter, joyous tears,
and a bag full of tangerines
beneath the clear blue skies
all overpower the concerns for what is to come.

Life is grand.

First Car
City Terrace, 1995

On their way home from school,
Walter and Junior find a hot pink
Power Wheel Barbie Corvette
without a battery alongside the road.

"It moves too slow," Junior says
"We gotta take out the gears."

"Yeah, and it's pink. We need to paint that shit.
I'm not gonna ride a pink car like a faggot,"
Walter adds.

Using our neighbor's tools,
my brothers pull out all the gears and wires,
cover the seats with masking tape
and newspaper, and give it a coat of primer.

While we wait for it to dry, we sit in the shade to share a
mango with lime and chili.
Once its finished,
we apply a coat of cherry gloss paint.

The next day, the car is ready to hit the streets.
We push it up the hill and let Junior take the first ride...
as if we had a choice.

I stand at the bottom, making sure no cars come
and, with a wave of my hand, give them the okay.
Walter gives Junior a push,
and momentum does the rest.

"Car!" my hands funnel my mouth to project my shout.

Junior is still racing down as the car approaches the intersection.

There's dread on Junior's face as he screams,
"Stop the car! We forgot the brakes!"

Walter chases after the runaway Corvette.
Junior starts zigzagging in an attempt to slow down
but spins out of control.
I wave, jump, and scream at the oncoming driver.

The driver honks and shouts, "Get out of the street!"

"Fuck you!" I reply,
flashing my middle finger as he drives off.

We learn nothing from Junior's near-death experience.
The only thing that can stop us
is the setting sun
or Mother coming home.

Family First
City Terrace, 1995

"Let's see who can climb that tree,"
suggests a friend of Junior's.

The first branch is too high.
No matter how good of a jumper you are,
it's always out of reach.

"We can give your little brother a boost
to get him up," suggest the brother of Junior's friend;
they're twins.

I hold onto Junior's shoulder with one hand,
place the other on the tree for balance,
and rest my right foot atop the twins' clasped fingers.
Three counts, and I'm up on the tree.

Everyone smiles,
celebrating the meaningless success.
When I look down, my fear of heights kicks in.
I hug the nearest branch and plead for
my brothers to help me down.

"Leave him up there," a twin scoffs.

I look at my brothers, waiting for them to help.
Instead they all start swinging dry branches at my
dangling feet and chanting, "Quiere llorar."

A few minutes pass, and they decide to stop.

Some people don't know any better,

but my brothers do.
Knowing this hurt more than the branches
marring my legs with bruises
and scratches that forced me to wear pants
for the next two weeks.

"Family first," I always hear people say.
I must not have been family that day.

Dinner Without Mother
City Terrace, 1995

Junior cooks for Walter and me.

In his culinary repertoire are
quesadillas,
Cup Noodles with lime and Tapatio,
sugar-dipped lime,
sour cream tacos with a pinch of salt,
or hotdog links charred on a fork over the stovetop.

This is dinner without Mother.
These days she is either working
or out dancing with friends.
This is life for years to come.

Eazy Rides

City Terrace, 1995

The blend of vanilla bean coffee creamer
and Aqua Net hairspray
fills the entire house
as we sit on the couch eating conchitas,
watching Chespirito.

My aunt combs my cousin's hair
with ponytails tight enough
to de-wrinkle the forehead of an eighty-year-old.
Her bald son, Lazy,
wears pants twenty-eight sizes too big
held up by a buckle belt
displaying the letter P in old English.
He's a cholo and a role model to me.

Two honks and a holler "Let's go!"
and seven kids, ages eight to thirteen,
jump into a three-seat Mitsubishi pickup truck—
two in the cab with the driver
and five on the flatbed with a camper.

Lazy doesn't put the truck in drive
until our morning anthem
"Real Mothafucken G's" is rattling every window.

Mother can't afford haircuts for all of us.
Junior is the only one to go to a barbershop.
Walter and I get haircuts at home—
a number one clip across our entire head.

Mother can't afford new uniforms for all of us.

Junior is the only one to get new uniforms.
Walter and I wear oversized hand-me-downs.

I look the part, and I play it even better.

Loneliness
City Terrace, 1995

Ice cream drips down cones,
seeps through napkins
and onto fingers.
We can't eat them faster
than the sun melts them.

Summer is coming to an end, and
we know this because
baseball season is already over.

We wash our hands with the water hose,
and Al says, "The berries are ready, guys.
We should go get some."

"How do you know, stupid?"
his younger brother asks.

"Because I passed by them yesterday, pendejo."

"Then go get some, joto. I'm not gonna go!"

They can go on like this for hours,
but Junior interrupts the discussion
to volunteer us both,
asking Al for a plastic bag.

Al smacks his brother on the back of the head
and orders him to get us one.

Between us and the tree,
there is an on old house on a hill

that everyone claims is haunted
after seeing medics carry a body out the front door.

My face tries to mask my fear,
but Junior picks up on it
and comforts me,
"It's not true. An old man lives there. I've seen him."

We climb down the first hill and
look up at the house.
"Go ahead. I'm right behind you," he says.

Trekking up the steep slope,
my eyes lock on the dingy blue door
with cracked paint hanging onto the walls
like leaves to branches of an autumnal tree.
The window sills, filled with webs,
are graveyards for flies.
Time and dust tint the windows.
The weeds surrounding the home
could erase anyone under four feet.

Underneath the tree, we pick foxtails from our socks
while our hearts resume a steadier rhythm.

"Climb up and grab as many as you can.
Only get the purple ones. The red ones aren't ready.
I'm gonna get the ones hanging low from the branches."

"Okay. I'll try to fill up the bag."

"Be careful with the ants."

We laugh and begin picking berries off their branches.

The drupes' skin—
supple, plump,
ready to burst—
must be picked softly
to avoid staining our clothes.

They are everywhere I turn—
above my head, below my feet—
staining dirt with a violet jam
for birds and ants to eat.

We've each filled up our bags about halfway
when we hear the gang
screaming from across the hill,
"Hurry up!"

Heading back, Junior decides
to cross the old man's yard
rather than to go around it.

"The back door is open!" he points out,
"I bet we can see him if we peek."

"Let's just go," I say. "Everyone's waiting."
My heart tugs me toward the stairs.

"He's watching TV!
I told you it wasn't haunted!"

My palms get sweaty,
my knees unsteady,
but I have to see for myself.

I walk over to the door,
peek my head in,

and suddenly feel a gust of wind
sweep over my face.
Junior had pushed me and ran off.
Panic strikes. I freeze for a moment,
but the pungent smell of urine and decay
cuts through the stillness.

I look around to see a box of rusting nails,
coffee mugs on every counter in sight,
piled dishes housing maggots and flies,
garbage-filled bags beside overflowing bins,
and, finally, there he was.

The man, wrinkled by time's careless crawl,
wearing a once-white button-up—
now a dingy yellow—
stares at the image of a women
in a dusty photo sitting above
his flickering television...
that seemed to be the only thing not frozen in time.

The phone rings, I jump,
and he doesn't even bother to turn.
The only call he is ready to answer is Death's.

He isn't scary at all.
Just alone.

1996-1999

Jumping for Joy
Mojave Desert, 1996

The alarm goes off at four in the morning.
My mother always showers first and then wakes my
brothers and me one by one by saying,
"Shower so we can leave on time."
She always does her makeup while we get ready
so we can be out of the door by 5:30 a.m.

We jump on a different freeway than normal.
I ask my mother why. To which she answers,
"They moved your dad a little further."

We drive about two hours to the Mojave Desert.
The doors open at eight.
We are one of the first families in line.
The trees stand naked.
The floor, covered with a thin film of ice,
entertains us during the wait.

The officer unlocks the door.
Mother fills out paperwork.
We're instructed to remove our jackets,
hats, belts, shoes, and lastly
empty our pockets onto the plastic trays before us.

I follow all orders but keep my shoes on.
When I walk up to the metal detector,
the officer asks me to remove my shoes again.
I refuse. When he tells my mother he will not allow us to
proceed,
my mother asks me what the problem is.

"My socks have holes," I respond.

She hugs me, tells me she has a surprise for me, and asks
me to listen to the officer.
I take my shoes off in embarrassment and walk through
the metal detector.

My brothers and I run around the waiting lobby while
mother makes change—
dollars to quarters—till a bus finally arrives on the other
side of the electric fences.

During the bus ride my mother smiles at us and says,
"This prison is a different than the last one.
You guys are gonna like it."

Walking onto the premises,
we see vending machines, microwaves,
tables, chairs, and even an outside patio area.
"Can we get some popcorn?" Junior asks.
"Here," she hands them the clear pouch full of coins.
"You and Walter go."
"Are you excited to see your dad?" Mother asks me.

"Yes. What's taking him so long?"

"Your dad isn't gonna be behind glass today. We aren't
gonna talk to him through a phone.
He'll come out, and you'll be able to hug him."

My eyes light up, and before
I even have the chance to reply,
my mother continues,
"Look! There he is."

I turn around to see him walking toward us.

"Dad!" I jump off my chair, run through the maze of tables, and leap into my father's arms.

I am seven-years-old, and it has been three years since I felt my father's embrace.

Hot Wheels and Solitude
City Terrace, 1996

Work, women, bb guns
and bike races
all rob me of my partners in crime.

There are days when
Walter gets home a little early,
and he jumps into the dirt mound with me.

"You have to put mud on your bridges,"
he explains as he mixes
a glass of water into a hole he dug.
"When it dries, it'll make them stronger."

On days like this
my brother and I stay outside
until the sun clocks out,
robbing banks and digging tunnels.

But for the most part,
at this point in my life,
my only friends are hot wheels and solitude.

Fishing
City Terrace, 1997

We stop by Big 5 Sporting Goods to
buy a six-pack of one-ounce weights,
two six-packs of size seven hooks,
and a two-hundred-foot roll of seven-pound test.
Afterward, Mother drives us to the beach.

Clad in worn-out hooded sweatshirts
and sweatpants over our jeans,
we walk onto Belmont Pier of Long Beach.

Mother tells each of us to quickly drink a can of Coke
while Junior runs to buy
a bag of anchovies from the bait shop.

"Watch how I do it, so you can make your own,"
she crunches the middle of the empty can,
runs the seven-pound test through the cap,
and ties a knot.
Turning the can sideways,
she wraps about forty feet of line around the can,
ties the weight to the end of the line,
and ties two hooks two feet apart from one another.

Junior arrives with the bait
as Walter and I set up our rigs.
Mother chops it up with a steak knife
and places a plastic bag over the frozen chunks
so the seagulls can't get to it.
After baiting her hooks,
she leans over the pier's railing, and
turns the can upright while holding the top.

She watches the weight unravel the line and
plunge into the sea.
You can taste the saltiness in the breeze coming in from
the horizon
where massive freight ships float by.

Ten minutes later, Mother catches our first fish, and
Junior is hooked.

Weekends

City Terrace, 1997

Every Monday the schoolchildren tell of
shopping malls, restaurants, and movie theaters—
weekend adventures.

My weekends are much simpler.

We either visit Father,
spending hours on the road,
or Mother drives us to Ecumex Video,
off 1st Street and Gage in East LA,
to rent some VHS movies
and walk over to 1st Street Burgers.

One dollar for a quarter-pounder
and a buck fifty for a giant scoop of steak fries.
The entire family eats for ten dollars.
Mother waits, tired in the car,
reminding us from the window
not to forget her yellow peppers.

We order four burgers and two fries
and use the change to buy
handfuls of M&M's or temporary tattoos.

Mother hates tattoos
—she ties them to cholos—
and always scrubs them off with a steel wool brush,
leaving my arm red for days.
It hurt like hell, but I get them anyway.

Driving home, we listen to Big Boy on Power 106,

eat loose fries out of the bag
and ignore Mother telling us to stop saying
"fuck," or "bitch."

We spread blankets on the living room floor,
eat our food, and fall asleep while watching movies.

We do not have much in comparison to others,
but Mother always finds a way to make it seem
like we have everything we could ever need.

Man Down
Geraghty Loma, 1997

My cousins and I play baseball
with a Wiffle bat and a plastic ball we stole
from the McDonald's ball pit.

Our strike zone is a tire on top of a milk crate.
Our field is a driveway
with broken red bricks for bases.
Branches cover most of the air space,
making it nearly impossible to hit a homerun.

As I'm standing on second base,
Junior releases the pitch
and Luis whacks that ball through the branches
and clean out of the driveway.

My gaze follows the ball rolling down the hill,
and I see a cholo exiting the passenger seat
of a car parked in the middle of the road.
He then walks over to a man
leaning on the hood of his car a little down the hill—
a close friend of the family—
draws a gun, and shoots him twice in the chest,
dropping him instantly.
Strutting backward, the cholo releases three more,
"P-taff! P-taff, p-taff!"

My aunt runs out, demanding that we get inside,
as the wailing man
screams for an ambulance.

She manages to gather us all inside

but only to find us with our noses pressing against the window.

The screams stop shortly after.
A local firefighter pronounces him dead,
and tears flood the streets he once walked upon.

Family Visits
Corcoran State Prison, 1997

Two-hour drives turn into four-hour ones.
One-hour visits once a month
turn into three-day visits
three times a year.

We have a home
to call our own,
all within
the prison walls.

Canned beef chunks and
Americas Most Wanted
every Friday
is our idea of family time.

Every night at 3:00 a.m.
the phone screams
through the steel cold walls,
waking everyone from their sleep.

It's check-in time for the inmate with no name.
He is only a number, another statistic, to them.

The rest of the weekend
my father teaches us math
and locks himself in the room
with our mother.

My brothers and I play handball,
prison style, and watch television.

When I get bored, I sit at the table
and draw in my prison cell.

Expulsion
City Terrace, 1998

"What happened, foo?!" Gus asks.

Gus is one of the few kids who gets me.
He grew up on the same hill as I did
and has culture running through his veins.

"Stupid Liz opened her fucken mouth," I reply.

"Your girlfriend, Liz?" he mocks me as I get up for a game
of handball.

Mid-game,
the principal comes up behind me and asks if we could
have a word.

"As soon as I lose," I reply.

He stands there several minutes as I play
before interrupting
to ask that I follow him to his office.

I tell him I don't want to go to his office.
He agrees to have our chat on a bench
away from classmates.

I tell him my point of view.
I tell him I am mad.
I tell him I want to be alone.

Then the first bell rings, telling students to get in line
and wait for their teachers.

"Let's go sit in my office, so you can calm down a little."

"I'm calm now. Can I just go back to class?"

He grabs my wrist and squeezes it.

I assume he's out of patience,
but Mother is the only human on the planet
to whom I grant permission to use force with me.

Not even my brothers hit me without taking a few slugs
in return.

I yank my arm and demand to be let go.
Once he notices other students watching him
drag me across the playground,
he releases me, and I fall onto the hot blacktop,
tearing a hole in my pants,
scraping my knee and palm.

I get up and run. He chases.

I hear the principal calling yard keepers for help.
I hear Gus cheering me on.
I hear every whistle on that playground going off.

As I run out of breath and slow down,
they close in on me.

The principal grabs both my arms
with a grip I can't shake,
and asks one of the yard keeps to grab my legs.
But he couldn't,
  so each one grabs an arm and a leg instead.

They carry me across the yard,
directly in front of where everyone lines up.

The ridicule overwhelms me.
Writhing, I manage to twist my right foot loose.
I swing it wildly,
knocking principal's glasses clean off his face.

The principal glares at me,
and there's a brief moment of silence
before the crowd goes wild.

The fight is over.
What I did is victory enough for me.
I surrender, letting them carry my limp body
into the building.

That night, my mother informs me of my expulsion.
I begin thinking of starting over in a new school
with no friends or family,
and my chin meets my chest.

For once, I have friends,
and I fucked it all up in a fit of rage.

Cans
Long Beach, 1998

Seagulls rob anglers of their bait.
Seals sway beneath the pier
as the sun falls into the horizon
and paints the ocean gold.

My aunt sits in her chair, knitting blankets.
My brothers fish, alongside my uncle and cousins.
I don't like fish and lost interest in the sport long ago.
So I sit there, eating the snacks my aunt packed,
talking to the anglers,
or playing Pokémon Blue Version
on a used Game Boy that Mother bought off my aunt.

"Are you ready?"
Mother looks to me with plastic bags in her hands.

"Yeah, Mom. Let's go," I smile.

"Junior and Walter, don't forget to help with all the stuff.
We'll wait for you in the car."

"Let's see who gets the most!"
she says, and I play along with her softness
as if I don't see her tactic.

We walk up to each and every trashcan,
remove the lid, search through fish guts
and leftover food,
and pick cans like fruit off a branch.

The people look at us sympathetically, and

some chug their drinks as they see us approaching.

"You're such a good boy for helping your mother,"
an old woman hands me a five-dollar bill.
"Buy yourself some candy."

My brothers walk by with hands full of gear,
asking Mother for the keys.
My aunt helps us,
so we can finish sooner and leave.
She doesn't like to leave without us.

I begin to understand
that Mother is struggling to keep us afloat;
it's why my brothers encourage stealing candy
rather than asking Mother to pay for it.

La Flor
Corcoran State Prison, 1998/1999

Father has big plans when he gets out.

He paints the dream of running a body shop,
just the two of us, where he can teach me
how to pull an engine apart and put it back together.
That, and getting us a house
where we won't all have to share a room.

Determined to do whatever it takes
to make things right,
he promises to cross the border after deportation
and work under a different social security number.

Mother and Father tell us
they want to have a daughter.
My brothers think a younger sibling is a great idea—
as if they don't already have one—
and I hate the idea of not being the youngest.
I even tell Mother I'll move to the dog house.

Father will be out in three years,
and he will finally have the chance to
watch one of his children grow up.

One month later,
Mother strides into our room, beaming.
We learn she's pregnant.
Five months later, we find out it's a girl.

The next time we have a family visit,
everyone writes a girl's name on torn pieces of paper.

We'll decide her name
by drawing one from a disposable cup.

I wrote Stephanie
—I've never met an ugly Stephanie—
and Father writes the word
"flower" in Aztec, Xochilt.

Mother slips her hand into the mouth of the cup,
grabs a piece of paper,
then reads us the verdict.

She's born in June 1999.
I'd never seen my mother so happy.

Mother works a job in embroidery.
Junior works construction.
Walter works at a summer camp.
And I sell candy at the park
during baseballs games that summer.

All so that we can provide the flower with
a nourishing environment in which to bloom—
something we don't have.

Middle School
East Los Angeles, 1999

Walter gives me a tour of the school.
Walking across the campus,
I notice people who love him,
mostly beautiful women
who enjoy stroking a boy's ego.

I also notice people who hate him,
mostly cholos with bald heads
and baggy clothing.

After the tour, he tells me that I'm not allowed
to hang out with him
or tell people he's my brother.

"It's for your own good,"
he gives me a shove,
"Go find your friends."

2000-2002

Writing for Fun
Belvedere Middle School, 2000

It's the last class of the day,
and the teachers are too lazy to teach a lesson.
At the end of every day,
they herd two classes into one room
and have us watch movies.

Since there aren't enough seats for all of the students,
some of us sit on the floor along the back wall.

There's a girl—very popular in our school—
who lets boys grope her for two dollars.

She's fully developed and always in short skirts,
but her eyes carry the sadness of a mourning widow.
One day after class, she lets it all out.

She confesses that her father molests and beats her;
has been doing it since she was six-years-old.
Her voice doesn't crack. She doesn't stutter.
The words numbly slip off her tongue
in a soft monotone
as her heavy eyes gaze forward,
and her mind moves backward
into the dark abyss she calls home.

Stopping me halfway down a flight of stairs,
she asks me to touch her as she lifts her shirt.

"I don't have any money," I say empathetically.

"It's okay. I like you," she studies my face

and rubs my crotch.

"It doesn't hurt my feelings. I like it now,"
she places my hand on her warm soft breast,
"I want you to; I promise."

I caress her breast, then her ass.
She smiles and kisses my cheek,
"You have a soft touch. Don't ever lose it."

Unequal Rights
City Terrace, 2000

I'm halfway through middle school,
and Mother starts giving my brothers
and me allowances—
Junior gets seven dollars per week,
Walter gets five, and I only get three.

"Why do I only get three dollars?!"
I ask mother ungratefully.

"Because you're smaller, that's why.
You don't need so much money."

I do not understand her logic—
a bag of chips and a can of soda cost the same
no matter how old you are.

Ripples
Laton, 2000 - 2001

It's summer vacation
and Mother is sending Walter and me up north
to bond with our long lost sister—
Father's firstborn—for a few weeks.

An excuse to get rid of us, but I don't blame her.

I've seen a picture of her, my older sister, once.
Purple bob cut, black lips and nail polish,
a nose piercing,
and our brown skin beneath layers of pale makeup.

Junior spoke to her on the phone once,
and she made a hell of a first impression.

"Hey, Junior! Do you know where you were seventeen
years ago?"

"Hmm, no. Why?" he replies.

"Well, I do," she says in between chuckles.
"You were in Dad's ball sack."
The dial tone rings in Junior's ear.

Her husband, Jim, is an ex-military drunk
who always stuffs snuff into his bottom lip
and responds like the asshole he is
to anything you say—
cool fucken guy.

They don't care to be normal, accepted,

and that's what I love most.

Jim hates people for the most part
and always talks about how his family hates him
for not being like his older brother.
And my sister, she's walking art.

With her arsenal of acrylic paints,
an acoustic guitar,
quiet nights, unlimited beer,
cigarettes, star-covered skies,
and a stash of porn under the sink
of the restroom where Jim's ex-wife hanged herself,
I form bad habits and new hobbies.

In their anarchy, I see courage.
In their madness, I feel acceptance.
In their home, I find myself.

Serpent Tongue
East Los Angeles, 2001

It hasn't even been a day, and she asks,
"Are you gonna kiss me?

I've never kissed a girl. Not even a peck.

My first relationship was in the fifth grade,
and all I ever did was gift her my snacks
and Looney Tunes stickers that I had doubles of.

She asks me to close my eyes
then shoves her serpent tongue in my mouth
and places my hands on her ass.

Her tongue, it moves in and out,
up and down, under and over.
It feels like I'm wrestling a gold medalist
inside my mouth.

We finish, and I can smell her saliva on my lips.
The pungent smell of shitty cafeteria corndogs
lingers in my nose
for the remainder of the school day.

Word spreads quickly, and I find out that
she cheated on me that day between classes.

She waits for me after school only to tell me,
"Well, I heard that you know I kissed someone
so I'm breaking up with you before you do."

"What a fucken bitch!" I think to myself.

"Alright," I learn to act and walk away.

This hurt,
it isn't like being punched in the face by Junior.
It feels more like a chisel
chipping away at my self-worth.

i wonder
where
the love went.

House Full of Strangers
City Terrace, 2002

Junior walks into the house, telling my cousin,
"We'll just do it in the restroom.
I don't want my aunt peeking out the window."
He moves between me and the TV I'm watching
to ask, "Have you ever smoked weed?"

"Yeah, man. A few times," I lie.

"Good. Then you can't fucken snitch.
Come on. We're gonna smoke."

Junior hands me the pipe and lighter.
My cousin sees that I have no idea what I'm doing.
"Cover the carp while you burn it," he explains.
"Then, release it
when you're ready to inhale the smoke.
Don't blow it out too soon!
Hold it in, or you won't get high."

I take a hit, inhale deeply,
hold it in, and begin to choke.

They laugh, calling me a rookie,
taking the pipe from my hand.

They ask if I'm high yet,
and I reply with a smile.
They laugh even harder.

"Remember when Walter thought
the TV was sucking him in?"

my cousin asks Junior.

"That's why I don't smoke with him anymore,"
he shakes his head in disappointment.
"He can't handle it."

They wander off into the screen.
I wander off into my mind,
and start thinking about how Junior is the perfect son
in Mother's eyes.

He goes to college.
He works and helps with bills.
He fills my father's shoes.
He keeps his troubles out of sight;
stashed in a tin behind all of his colognes.

The Taste of Freedom
Tijuana Mexico, 2002

Ten years of waiting. Over.
The sheriff's bus kicks up dust
as it pulls into the terminal.
A guard steps out and releases
the inmates one by one.
Father's foot lands on his motherland,
and he smiles without restraint.

For ten years the man was told what to eat.
For ten years the man was told where to be.
For ten years the man was told when to wake.

"I want some fucken birria,"
he releases after greeting everyone.

As he sinks his teeth into a tortilla hecha a mano
dripping with the birria sauce,
a tear of joy falls from his left eye.
I'm the only one to notice.
He wipes it off before anyone else can see.

The weekend is filled with eating Mexican delicacies—
pozole, tamales, elote, tacos al pastor, chilaquieles—
but, most of all,
we overindulge in each other's company
without undergoing complete scrutiny.

He is free.
In a way, so are we.

2003

Some Things Never Change
Puerto Nuevo, 2003

Walter flies into Tijuana
after spending a few months with Father in Guadalajara.
Father's smile seems heavier than Walter's
oversized luggage.

That night my brothers and father
go for a walk on the beach
with nothing more than a twelve pack in hand.

I ask Mother if everything is okay.
She lights a cigarette and sends me to bed.

The next morning,
I find Father sleeping on the couch
and Mother drinking a coffee on the front patio.

Without having breakfast,
we all walk to the beach
and lay out a blanket to sit on.

A man selling jewelry comes up to us,
and I ask Father to buy me a silver ring
with a peace sign on it.
He grunts but agrees.

"Are you ready?" Mother asks my father.

His silence speaks for him.
Mother then causes ripples,
"Me and your dad agreed that
it's best if we go separate our ways.

He's going to live in Mexico.
He'll still call and write.
You guys can come visit him whenever you want.
I will never come between you all."

He sits there, only managing to utter,
"You guys can come to see me in TJ.
I just can't go back to the states.
If I get caught, I'll go back to prison.
You all know that."

The ripples become waves
that crash hard against my mind—
Why make Mother wait ten years?
Why feed me all of those false promises?
Why agree to have a daughter
if you knew you weren't going to stick around?
Why cower away after everything we've done?
Why act like you have a heart?
But there is no answer that will satisfy me.
So I hold onto the questions
and file them under "unanswerable."

I feel what's left of my innocence dying.
I feel anger overpowering pain.
I watch my dreams slip away with the tide.

Reality
Guadalajara/ Michoacán, 2003

Father and I arrive at Villa Victoria
after a long drive from Guadalajara.

I walk into the house I am to sleep in—
desolate, cold, unfurnished.

There are rumors that my father
has an eighteen-year-old girlfriend.
He denies this to me repeatedly
but sleeps at her house every night.

I came to spend time with my father
but end up sleeping alone
on an old mattress with a gun under my pillow.

He doesn't have time for his son.
His words are as genuine as
the ring decaying my finger.
He doesn't fear getting caught in the U.S.;
he just has a new, younger, dream.

Yesenia
Villa Victoria, 2003

I'm fourteen-years-old;
a grown man in a place like this.

I spend my days with the pueblos children.
We go hunting for iguanas in the forest,
using only pebbles and slingshots.

I spend my afternoons with my newfound cousins.
We drink till the sun falls
into the mountains behind us,
then watch a man turn on every light post
so that the pueblo isn't engulfed by darkness.

The nights are quiet,
and the moon floats across the sky
with the company of ten thousand stars
beneath which Yesenia and I sit.

We met at a small restaurant
where she works as a waitress.
I make sure to be there every night before they close
just to walk her home.

Sometimes we sit on a bridge,
feet dangling,
and talk about the sadness in my eyes
or the life behind her smile.

There is care in her ardent stare.
There is calm in her gentle touch.

One night, after planting a kiss on my cheek,
she asks me to stay in Mexico,
and I feel the fragility of her vulnerable heart.

Now my afternoons slip into
unholy hours of the night,
and in place of her warm hand, I hold cold beers.

I see her one night while driving with my cousin.
She looks me dead in the eye then turns away.

I jump off of my cousin's truck at the next stop sign,
and walk up to her.

I smile, and she turns red.

"Where have you been?" she folds her arms.
"Are you high?"

"I know that I can't stay here,
and I don't want to hurt you,
but I know that I'll miss you when I leave."

"It's too late," pushing me aside.
"You've already left."

"Don't worry," my cousin consoles me
as I jump back into the passenger seat.
"There are plenty of sluts out here.
You don't need her."

La Cascada
El Salitre, 2003

It's my last week in Mexico,
so my cousin organizes a trip to the waterfall
with a group of girls and a few quarts of Mescal.

We drive around the mountain
and arrive at El Salitre.

We trek for two hours,
crossing the river several times,
climbing boulders and rocks,
dodging branches and wasps.

The waterfall cascades from eighty feet above us.
The women radiate drunken delight.
I feel alive and nothing hurts—
not the freezing cold water that pricks my back like tiny
cactus spines,
not the weight of knowing about
my father's new life,
not the turmoil I carry inside.

Real Men

Michoacan, 2003

We drive around looking for a good place to eat.

"How did you like your trip?" my cousin asks.

Gazing out of the window, I reply, "It was cool."

"I bet you saw a lot of shit you didn't expect.
Like your dad working...and his girlfriend."

"Yeah. I thought the guy would have learned his lesson
after spending ten years in prison, but I guess I was
wrong."

"You know you can't tell your mother right?"

"I wasn't planning on it."

He pulls off to the side of the road, and
placing his hand on my shoulder, he says,
"I mean it. You'd break her heart. You love her, right?"

"More than anyone."

"Then you don't want to hurt her."

"I already told you. I'm not gonna say anything."
"Good. Because that's what real men do."

Putting the car back into gear,

he continues,
"We look out for each other,
and we only lie to the women we love
because we don't want to hurt them.
We don't need to go through
that kind of trouble for our girlfriends.
As long as we fuck them
and buy them nice things, everything is fine."

Last Goodbye
Michoacan/ Guadalajara, 2003

As I pack my bags and vices,
Father spends the day with his lover.

My bus arrives. I get a one-handed hug,
two-thousand pesos for a plane ticket, and
a "take care."

I ride on a dirt road for the first two hours.
The road is two feet wider than our bus,
and I fear falling off the edge,
especially after the driver stops and we all drink
pajaretes.

After arriving at my uncle's mansion,
he takes one look at me and says,
"Cut that hair off. You look like a girl."

I shake my head from side to side.

"I'll pay you three hundred dollars to cut it,"
he pulls the money out of his wallet and tosses it on the
coffee table.

I shake my head from side to side
and walk away with my dignity.

His money controls the world he lives in.
I wonder how he feels being powerless for a moment.

When I get back home two weeks later,
I pay seven dollars to cut it all off.

It's too hot to bear,
but the choice is mine.

Troubles

City Terrace, 2003

Mother smokes two cigarettes a day after work,
sitting out on the front porch,
staring out into the distance.

This ritual lasts several months.

Walter and I raid Mother's stash
every night when she falls asleep.

She keeps the cigarettes on top of the fridge,
behind the bags of chips and Oreos.

Fresh fruit is rare in our household now.
Go-Gurt, Jell-O,
and anything else that doesn't perish easily
fills our fridge.
No one has an appetite for things that can go bad.

Swinging on a hammock beneath the mispero tree,
we share a smoke,
and talk about troubles with breathing.

We both see things differently after going to Mexico,
and neither of us care to speak of it with anyone else.

This ritual lasts several years,
and it only gets worse as time drags us on.

Junior and Mother claim they saw my father's departure
coming;
but that's bullshit.

Every one of us is hurting.
There is no longer a bigger picture to look towards.
There is only the mess he made
that he expects Mother to clean up.

2004-2005

Cop Ride
City Terrace Park, 2004

"Alright, who is smoking?" the officer asks.
"We thought it was weed, but who has the cigarettes?
Come on.
Don't make me search all of you."

I was the only one smoking,
and I know my friends have weed.
I'm not about to let them go down because of me.

"I do," I reply
after tossing my pocketknife onto the grass.

"How old are you, kid?"

"Seventeen."

"Seventeen? You know you have to be eighteen to smoke,
right?"

"Yeah."

"Alright, let's go for a ride."

We drive around the park.
He asks why I smoke and then my age again,
tells me my friends are bad influences,
then stops in the middle of the baseball field
to stare me down through the rear view mirror,
"How old are you really?"

"Seventeen."

"You're only getting a warning 'coz you're being honest,
you hear me? Just 'coz you're being honest."

He knows I'm lying,
but he also knows I won't change my story.

He calls my mother to pick me up,
then asks her for my age.
She plays along.

My first thought upon seeing her is,
"I'm going to boot camp."

She threatens me with it often
but never follows through.

On the ride home,
Mother asks if it is me stealing her cigarettes.

I tell her it is.

She doesn't yell at me.
She just sits in silence
as worry curtains her tired eyes.

Cravings
City Terrace, 2004

Father never calls.

Mother finds new love,
as she has the right to,
and my brothers and I hardly talk.

Our home is in pieces.

We live in a one-bedroom apartment.
There is nowhere to sit and think.
There is always someone watching television
or listening to music.

All I crave is stillness.

I clean out a three-by-seven
shed in front of our home,
put an old desk in it, and begin
to unscramble my thoughts.

I understand that death can take
our loved ones away—
it took my grandmother
before I got the chance to know her—
but it is life that took my father from us,
and now it is taking my mother.

Broken Nose
City Terrace, 2004

Mother opens the package addressed to her
and pulls out a Led Zeppelin Zippo lighter.

"Did you order this?" she asks.

I tell her I didn't.

"It has your fucken name engraved on it!" she continues.
"Junior!"

"What happened?"
Junior walks in the house.

"Your brother ordered this lighter with my credit card!"

Mother might as well have said, "Sick'em, boy!"

Junior pushes me into our bedroom
and pins me against the wall.

BAM!
I block the first punch with my forearm.
BAM! ...BAM! CRACK!
The last two land dead on my nose.

Junior's face goes from furious to concerned
and from concerned to ashamed in seconds.

"You see what you made me do?
You stupid piece of shit,"
he barks as the rabies-like froth drips from his mouth.

"Fuck you, Junior!" I reply
before spitting a mouth full of blood at his face.

He storms out.

Mother screams franticly when she sees me.

I walk past her and into the restroom
without saying a word.

Looking into the mirror, I see my nose is swollen
and leaning to the left.
Tears of rage run down my face.
I close my eyes
and pop it back into place using mothers lip liner.

I feel no pain.
The adrenaline is still pumping. All I feel is anger.

The next day Mother drives me to the hospital.
The nurse asks what happened.
I tell her I fought a stranger, and Mother smiles.

.

Blue

Lincoln Heights, 2005

I fell, like a tree chopped from its base.

My vision comes and goes,
but I can still hear everything.

I hear the kids running and playing.
I hear an ice cream truck in the distance.
I hear Walter calling out for Mother as he and my cousin
carry my limp body towards her.

"What the fuck did you guys give him!?"
my godfather asks as he and Mother walk to me.

Mother lifts my cold face with her warm hands
and begins slapping me, asking me to wake up.

After loading me onto my aunt's truck,
Walter waves a t-shirt soaked in rubbing alcohol
under my nose, and my cousin slaps me repeatedly
until I regain consciousness.

My opening eyes lock onto the rear view mirror—
pale blue skin, plum purple lips,
bloodshot crimson eyes.

As we walk into the hospital,
my cousin warns me to deny everything.

The doctor asks what happened.
I tell her that I tripped
over the wire of a Play Station controller.

She waits until Mother leaves the room
before saying,
"I don't know what you're going through,
but drugs aren't the answer.
You didn't fall.
We instinctually break our falls with arms outstretched.
There is no sign of that.
You were out cold before you hit the ground.
This time you only got stitches.
Next time could be a lot worse."

Green-Eyed Love Spell
Woodrow Wilson, 2005

I'm waiting for a friend, and apparently, this girl is
waiting for him, too.

She's strange—choppy greenish hair she cuts herself,
a teal t-shirt that complements her nice tits,
green eyes with hints of honey
and auburn around the pupils,
leopard print patches on her pants, shoes, and jacket.

"Stop trying to steal my friend,"
she disturbs the awkward silence, laughing.
"Sorry for talking to you. What's your name?"

Girls at my high school flirt with giggles and smiles.
This gal, she's different.

There is gauze wrapped around her left wrist,
and I ask what happened.

She dodges the question
and jokes about my shirt that reads:
"Mr. Pecker's Rooster Farm.
We have the biggest cocks in town."

Junior bought the shirt for my birthday.
He found a new girlfriend.
She seems to make him more human than asshole.

Moments later, our friend walks out,
and the dick tells me he isn't going home.
He's going to her house

so she can sew in his already tight pants.

It sounds like bullshit to me.
I convince myself they're fucking.

Walking to the bus stop,
I see a cute girl from my first period sitting alone.

I sit beside her, and we talk.

She giggles frequently
and keeps shifting her gaze
from my eyes to my lips.
Nothing I hadn't seen before.
Nothing like those green eyes.

Momma's Boy
Woodrow Wilson, 2005

The problem is
that most people like to open their big mouths.
And me, well,
I like to make sure they learn when to keep it shut.

This is the third time Mother leaves work
to pick me up from school for being suspended.

The car doors slam, seat belts click,
she turns off the radio,
and in her softest voice asks,
"What happened this time?"

"He talked bad about you,"
I respond with my head down.

"He doesn't know me!
Why would you let that bother you?
He could think and say whatever he wants!"

This is where I disagree.
I never believed that "sticks and stones" bullshit.
To me, words are powerful.
That's why lies leave scars.

"When are you going to learn to listen?
I'm tired of this! I don't know what to do anymore!"
taking a heavy breath mid-rant, she continues,
"I want to help you, but I can't if you don't let me. Why
do you push me away?"

I have answers. I choose not to voice them.
I don't know how to tell her that I miss who she was
before my father left.
I don't know how to tell her that I hate the fact that she
has a boyfriend.
I don't know how to tell her about the emptiness I feel
within.

"One more suspension or phone call from Mr. Guzman,
and I'm putting you in homeschool.
Is that what you want?!"

"No, Mom."

"You make me feel like giving up. I don't want to give up
on you!" she cries.

I hug her.

"Don't worry about me, Mom. I'll be all right."

She doesn't say another word.
She just turns the car on and drives away.

The whole ride home I feel like telling her about
everything that is eating away at my joy.
But I don't. I can't.
These walls I've built won't let me.

Good Mornings

El Sereno, 2005

After getting dropped off at school, I walk over to her
house.

She lives four blocks away
and doesn't have a first or second period.

I hush the dogs, walk in through the side gate,
quietly climb into her window, kiss her cheek,
kick off my shoes, and lie beside her.

Some days we sleep, others we have sex—
she is my first love, the gal with the green eyes.

Some days we just lie there,
running fingers up and down ribs,
over and across abdomens,
spilling secrets and fears
'till we have to go back to school.

Other days we stay in our own little world
where no one could bother us, doubt us, or judge us.

She's broken, but I don't care. I am just as damaged.
The only difference is no one can see my scars,
I bury them beneath a smile,
and she wears hers on her sleeve.

I know she is fragile.
I know she thinks it makes her weak.
I know that behind all those awkward jokes

there is a girl who just wants to be loved for something other than her body.

I also know that I can do exactly that.

Gigs

El Sereno, 2005

Three dollars at the door,
one twenty-five for a Black & Mild,
and two dollars for a forty oz. Miller Highlife—
my seven-dollar allowance covers my vices.

Cute girls in fishnets and short skirts,
reefer, meth, Djarums,
and any other smoke you can imagine
fills the air we breathe.

The girls, both drunk and horny,
grabbing cocks like fiends,
hope you have a van or car to fuck them in.

The boys, both drunk and full of testosterone,
mosh around a pit like bulls in a ring.

Everyone knows we only have 'till ten—
midnight the latest—
before the cops show up.

So we all drink quickly to get our buzz going.

My girlfriend kisses other girls,
and all the guys cheer her on.

She doesn't understand why I'm upset—
every other guy seems to be impressed
by her actions.

To me, she isn't one of those sluts

that fuck random guys in the back of cars.

To me, she is soft and vulnerable...
and courageous for being so.

As the days roll on,
I realize she is far from the girl I imagined her to be;
but it's too late to walk away unscathed.
I love her and her fucked up ways.

2006

Absent Love
City Terrace, 2006

Her smile has been gone for weeks,
and she leaves to her mother's house
every chance she gets.
She's always told me she hates it there.

There is no silencing the suspicion.
It robs me of peace.
She says I'm being paranoid.
I say she's being distant.

Weeks later, a mutual friend breaks the news.
It's amazing...the way it doesn't immediately hurt.
I hear the same happens when someone gets shot.

I've forgiven her kissing other men,
but this is deeper.
There is emotional attachment.
Being drunk is no longer a permissible excuse.

The hardest part isn't seeing the proof in pictures.
The hardest part is looking at those pictures and finding
everything that has been missing—
her love, her passion, her smile.

The hardest part isn't finding out that this is no secret—
all of our friends have known for months.
The hardest part is packing all of her belongings into a
black duffle bag and realizing
that the only thing getting heavier is my heart.

02/11/06

Skin and Bones
City Terrace, 2006

"You're getting skinny,"
my drunk aunt reproaches me.

"He skates a lot,"
my mother quickly defends.
"He comes home every day drenched in sweat."

I haven't skated in weeks.
Mother should know this,
but she's too busy playing house.

"Yeah...I skate a lot,"
I smirk at my aunt and raise my beer for a cheers.

She doesn't really care to know what's wrong.
She just wants something to talk about.

I don't talk to anyone about my problems—
insomnia, lack of appetite, cocaine –
or the reasons behind them.

Instead, I stay up all day and night in my little shack,
drinking, smoking, snorting,
writing about the effects of abandonment.

Confidant
Echo Park, 2006

She asks why I feel so much anger toward my family.

"I don't. I just don't think they care."

She asks why I took so many pills.

"I just wanted to sleep."

She asks what I've been writing about.

"The emptiness inside all of us that we try to fill."

She asks if I still talk to my ex and then asks why.

"I miss her. I still want her.
She says she still loves me."

She asks what makes me happy.

"Writing, painting, collaging,
any form of creating, really."

She asks if I still have suicidal thoughts.

"I didn't try to kill myself. I just wanted to sleep."

Sympathy
Everywhere, 2006

Everyone cares now.
Everyone tries to help.
Everyone is extra nice.
Everyone tries to spend time with me.
Everyone wants to pull me out of my head.
Everyone worries about me.
Everyone knows what is best for me.
Everyone treats me like a ticking time bomb.

New World
El Sereno, 2006

"You've always looked like a good fuck,
not someone I'd be with,"
the gal says as we sit on Mother's couch.

I act like it doesn't bother me
and begin kissing her neck.

As I make my way down to her chest,
I hear my mother's van pulling up,
and the gal looks down at me in disappointment.

She puts her glasses back on,
tucks her breast back into her bra,
and we begin playing FIFA.

Mother walks in, tired as always,
giving me a look that shouts,
"Another one!?"

The gal introduces herself to my mother,
very ladylike—
she isn't fooling anyone in that short skirt.

My mother, being the angel that she is,
greets her with respect, then walks to her room.

I want to give this woman more than an orgasm,
but at this point, I find myself
in a world where the notion of finding love
is farfetched.

The only way to feel anything
is by fucking, using, or drinking.

Price of Freedom
El Sereno, 2006

I'm only seventeen and a half.
Junior and I decide to move out
of our mother's house
and into a two-bedroom garage.
All for the sake of doing what we please
when we please.

The walls in our new house don't reach the ceiling.
Our rooms look more like cubicles.
I could hear Junior fucking, shitting, living.

I get a job unloading trailers
at the Macy's distribution center on Broadway
to pay my half of the rent.

I wake up to an alarm at 4:30 a.m.,
take a shower if I'm not too tired,
fix my coffee to-go, and drink it on the road.

I clock in for work at 5:15 a.m.,
break my back
with men twice my age
who advise me to run while I still can,
who warn of the quicksand
beneath our feet and
the inevitable outcome of a life without dreams.

They talk about a never-ending continuum
of work and catching up on overdue bills,
a never-ending continuum of nagging women
and limp dicks,

because once you marry
the fucking stops,
and once the fucking stops
you lose the passion,
then the blood slows down to a crawl,
and you're as good as dead.

2007

Moving Up
Lincoln Heights, 2007

Promotion. Raise. Graveyard shift.
No more lifting heavy boxes with old, bitter men.

All I have to do is sit on my ass
and try not to fall asleep.

Read a little, write a little,
and try not to fall asleep.

Take a smoke break, fix another coffee,
and try not to fall asleep.

Watch the cameras, take a walk,
be on the lookout for suspicious activity
or people fucking in parking lots,
but, most importantly,
try not to fall asleep.

Hold my head up until the sun rises,
then let it fall onto my pillow.
I convince myself the sun is overrated anyway.

Optimism, you're killing me.

Drunken Loneliness
El Sereno, 2007

Bellies fill with liquid courage.
Minds fly dangerously high.

Women laughing,
fucking me from across the room,
wondering why I don't go say hello.

I have a great fear of rejection,
so I never do.

Instead, I stumble from place to place.
Looking for a chair or a ledge
where I can rest my feet
so they cease fighting
to keep the rest of me off the ground.

"Are you okay?"
the pretty redhead asks.

I look up at her with one eye open.
"Why?"

"You look really fucked up,"
she says while taking my cigarette
from between my lips.

"I am fucked up.
All kinds of fucked up."

"What are you on?"

"Well, I'm drunk, high, lonely, horny,
most of all, I think, I'm a little fucken crazy."

She laughs and smiles,
"I think you're funny."

"I think you're horny...
or crazy. One or the other."

"Maybe a little of both."

We talk for about an hour
before we walk to the liquor store
for more beers and cigarettes.
We fuck in an alley on the way back,
walk into the party,
and don't speak again
...just share a smile goodbye.

Thieving Currents
El Sereno, 2007

Lonely hearts always ask where I am going,
but I have no idea,
so I answer with the only truth I hold, "Nowhere."

I make my way through the emptiness,
riding treacherous waves that only crash
on the beds of lonesome lovers.

Lying naked, exposed, vulnerable, and brave,
we laugh, sigh, kiss, and cry,
letting out all the pain,
hoping to stop it from eating us within.

Running my calloused fingers down steep hips,
I sometimes feel love on the other side
of my thick skin
as the dame rests her heavy head on my quiet chest.

It is in these moments
that happiness finds me briefly,
when silence does not feel like a burden
but, rather, more like a cocoon weaved for two
made of a silky surrender and victory.

There are no promises to be broken
in the space between the sunken sun
and the moonless night.

Everyone here understands the riptides—
they are strong enough to loosen grips—
and that is enough to keep half smiles alive,

and that is enough to say goodbye without a fight.

Torn apart and put back together by the same force,
I ebb and flow between
 the mournful cries of loneliness
and the serenading peace I hear only in solitude.

All that is left of me is a man dying of thirst,
floating in saltwater,
too smart to drink,
yet too tired to swim against the thieving currents.

Empty Full House
El Sereno, 2007

Women fill every room of our house.
Drinks overflow the brims of cups
onto filthy linoleum floor.
Music bounces off walls
and into ears that never learned to listen.
Smoke fills the atmosphere and my lungs.

I'm filling empty conversations.
I'm suffocating in societal acceptance.
I'm growing out of this me.

Disconnected
El Sereno, 2007

No social media, no television,
no radio stations, no cell phone,
no influences from the outside world.

I spend my evenings reading,
smoking, painting, writing, skating,
and loving casually.

I'm finding myself in this solitude.
I can't afford to get attached.
Not after freeing myself from others' expectations.

Surviving

El Sereno, 2007

I look at the world
through the fissures of this broken heart
and realize we aren't living.

I see the overwhelming burden of this game of life
through the eyes of a single mother
who is forced to leave her infant at home
in order to work and provide.

I see the exhaustion of the elderly man
pushing an elote cart up a steep hill,
breaking a sweat and also his back
in his attempt to save his children from a similar fate.

Sleep, work, cook, eat, shit, shower, sleep.
Repeat for seventy years.
This is all most of us will see.
This is all most of us will know.

The grass on our side of town
is its last shade of yellow— borderline dead.

The only place it grows greener
is where our people get paid to maintain it.

That Something
El Sereno, 2007

The only time we exchange words
is when she asks for permission to paint on my walls,
and I respond with a calm "Go for it."

Her smile exudes happiness,
but holds longing,
the same longing I see in my own reflection.

I need to know if the mushrooms are kicking in
or if our souls are dancing on a higher plane.

Conversations with the Night
El Sereno, 2007

On nights like this, still,
I drown in memories;
but she makes them bearable.

She never does much, but she listens.
She is there, always,
and that is doing more than anyone has.

We smoke. We talk. We kiss.
We make love and share my twin size bed.

5 a.m. always comes too soon.
She leaves at this time to take her mother to work,
only to come back at 8 so we can sleep until 11.

On mornings like this—euphoric—we roll in sheets
and plan a life where we don't have to leave each other
every night.

She loves me, and I don't understand why.
I love her, and it terrifies me.

She doesn't make my heart palpitate.
On the contrary, she slows it down,
along with my mind and life.

The Fear of Failure

El Sereno, 2007

What if she hurts me?
What if she tires of me?
What if she leaves me sitting on this cloud alone?
Why grow attached to something that can leave?
Why risk all of the possible pain?

Solitude has never hurt me.
Loneliness is gone.
I'm fine on my own.
Love is O-1.
And I'm not sure I'm willing
to gamble on those odds.

But then she looks at me,
and I forget how to do math.

I Do Not Belong
El Sereno, 2007

Attempting to avoid conflict in life,
I bite my tongue.

They make me feel mad when I say
I see lust sold as love.

They make me feel stupid when I say
I see ignorance sold as bliss.
They make me feel like I don't belong when I say
I see that the world is under a spell.

The things "they" represent
are what stings me.

"They" are everyone in my life—
family, coworkers, old friends.

I try so hard to open their eyes,
to be the bucket of ice cold water
that shocks them from deep sleep.

I try so hard to get them to see that I care for them,
but in this life, you only make friends by agreeing.

Instead of trying so hard to prove them wrong,
I should be listening to the truth
they're spitting in my face.

I don't belong in their world.

It's obvious,

I belong in one that allows digression.

2008-2009

Big Brother
El Sereno, 2008

The masses are studied like lab rats.

Serve them shit for ninety-nine cents,
see if they'll eat it.

Feed them entertainment as news,
see if they'll believe it.

Collect information!
All information!
We need to know everything!
What they love.
What they hate.
What they buy.
What makes them laugh.
What makes them cry.
What they fear.
What they fear.
What they fear.

The Glory
El Sereno, 2008

Infatuation with opulence is
instilled in the minds of the people.

Programming takes place daily.
Tune into the norm's wavelength.

Sit—stuck on the screen and couch—
for hours at a time,
soaking your mind in frames of fame,
fear, and fortune.

Sit—stuck in traffic and life—
detached from your mind,
distracting your thoughts with the sounds of partying,
sex, and gossip.

Sports cars. Mansions. Diamonds.
Everything is plastic—
smiles, tits, hearts, and intentions.

The glorified dollar equates to happiness...
only to those who have nothing of higher value.

Let's Build a Home
Monterey Park, 2009

Working isn't my favorite thing to do—
not because I'm lazy,
but because time, to me,
is more precious than money.

But I do it anyway
in the name of our dream.

We need a TV with which to watch movies,
a nicer couch, a dining table,
a computer, a desk, a new dresser, a rug,
a shower curtain, new sheets, new pillows,
new blankets, a vacuum, pots, pans, cups, plates,
bowls, spoons, forks, knives,
picture frames for my posters,
and a shelf for my records because
she hates the way my milk crates look.

Now we can sit here and enjoy it all.
As long as we're not too loud.
As long as we hold our jobs.
As long as we both shall live.

.

Past in Present
Monterey Park, 2009

It kills me.

The way her eyes smile at strangers
the same way they once smiled at me.

The way they insist on conversation
and suggest compliments.

The way they gaze at everything i am not—
"manly," tall, educated, normal.

It kills me.

The way my mind runs toward memories
that i cannot rid myself of.

The way they remind me
that i am still not worthy of love.

The way they close me, numb me,
and walk me to the nearest liquor store.

Safety Nets
Monterey Park, 2009

Stagnancy. Complacency. Squandering feelings.

We fight more than we make love.
Our insecurities are airing.

We don't make the time to make up.
Our defenses are strengthening.

This dream is unstable.
My eyes can see us falling apart
a few miles up the road.

I must cushion the fall.
I must find a way to stay intact
when I fall out of this love
and crash hard against the ground.

Mistakes

Monterey Park, 2009

I know what must happen now.

I need to move out.
I fucked up.
You won't trust me anymore.
Your heart will declare a war on our love.

I'm sorry, but I can't stay and watch you hurt.

Pride
Commerce, 2009

Covered in dust and grime,
I walk up to the parking structure.

To my surprise,
there you are, my love, wearing a smile.

"What are you doing here?"
I ask while looking around
to make sure the other woman doesn't pull up.

"I knew you were getting off right now.
I thought maybe you'd like a ride.
Let's go eat and talk?" the angel sings.

"I'm sorry, I can't.
I already made plans..."

"Don't be this way. I really miss you."

"Get out of here," I demand,
"We can't fix what I broke. Trust me.
You're only gonna hurt more."

"You're so fucken cold," she cries.
"I'm trying to fix things because I love you.
Why can't you see that!?"

"Look, I'm no good for you. Trust me."

"If you want to talk, I'll be home.
Come by. Come back already. I miss you."

Inseparable
Monterey Park, 2009

I love you in a way I've never loved.
Fearfully.

I take cautious steps and heed red flags—
the way you ignore my desperation calls
but hold your phone more
than my hand when you're with me,
the way we've only had sex once
in the past two months,
the way you walk into another room
to reply to text messages,
or the way there's a space that sits between
our meeting lips.

You care. Of this, I am certain.

But you lie.
You lie about where you've been.
You lie about who you've been with.
You lie about your love for me.

If it is gone, tell me.
I cannot blame you.
I made the mess in this heart.

It's been two years.
On and off.

You move in. You move out.
And this time around,
I am certain you've moved on.

Bittersweet

Monterey Park, 2009

She texts me, "I miss you."

I immediately reply, "I love you."
I wasn't sure of this then,
but I'm sure of it now.

"Help me wash my car?"

Of course I don't want to,
but I know it was an excuse,
and it's good enough for me.

I've been waiting for this day—
the day she opens up and lets me back in,
the day I can hold her—
because I've learned not to let her go.

I ride my bike five miles to her house,
carrying a letter that I wrote her days ago
and a small bouquet of white roses
that I stole from my neighbor's garden.

We greet with a hug—
the kind of hug you soak in,
the kind of hug that says,
"Don't push me away."

I walk inside for a towel after washing the car
and hear the bleep
of an incoming text message on her phone.

Glancing at it,
I see the recipient's name, "ZZZZZZ."

This is the first time she doesn't have her phone
locked away in her purse or in her hand.

Every part of my being tells me
to open the message, so I do.

"Babe it was nice seeing you last night
I hope to see you again tonight."

Last night
she bailed on me last minute.
Last night
she said she was having dinner with her sister.
Last night
I hated myself for doubting her,
for thinking so little of her.

Today I learn to trust my intuition.

A Reason to Return
Monterey Park, 2009

"I haven't had my period this month,"
she looks me dead in the eyes.
"I'm two weeks late."

"Why are you telling me this?"
I snap. "Shouldn't you be telling your new man?"

"I'm telling you because it can only be yours."

"You're telling me that you haven't had sex with your
guy?"

"Honestly, no I haven't."

I know she's lying.
Her face tries hard to act natural.
Her voice tries hard to sound convincing.

"Well, let's go buy a test and find out for sure."

We drive to Rite Aid in Atlantic Square
and buy two tests.

I know she's afraid.
Her breath tries hard to be steady.
Her eyes try hard to look past this day.

"Okay. I'm gonna do it,"
she walks into my mother's bathroom.

Sitting in the living room, I start thinking of everything
I'd do if she is pregnant.
My mind has never gone down this path.

She walks out, smiles nervously, and begins to cry.

I stand, hold her snug in my arms,
and reassure her.

I'll take care of us—
the three of us.

2010

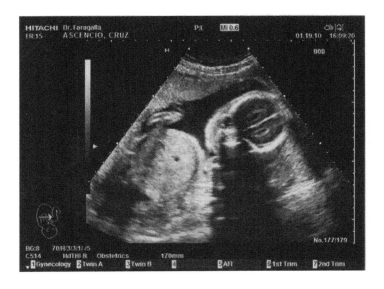

The Closest Thing to Happiness
Alhambra, 2010

Slowly but surely, we gather everything he'll need—
crib, stroller, car seat, bottles, pacifiers,
blankets, clothes, diapers, wipes, toys,
and, most importantly,
a home with both of his parents.

I work two jobs to keep us warm.

She takes care of our space,
herself, and our unborn son.

I've given up alcohol for over six months.
I quit after going to jail for public intoxication.
I got into a brawl with half of my cousins.
My mother and girlfriend called the cops on me,
fearing what I was capable of.
I know the power my rage can have over me.
I hold no resentment for what they did.

Now, we've never been so steady.
Maybe it was my alcoholism
that caused all of our problems.

Arguments are nonexistent,
and I could feel her love again.
I feel it in every kiss hello and goodbye.
I feel it in every home-cooked meal.
I feel it in the way she rests her head on my shoulder
while we watch countless movies.

I do what I can to make sure she's better than good.

Like run to the store at midnight
because she craves a Reese's Cup.
Like make sure we take a walk every day
because these are the doctor's orders.
Like go to every single appointment,
so she knows we're in this together.

We made it.
We broke the cycle of breaking homes.
Our son will grow up
understanding what it means to be loved.

Truth Kills
Alhambra, 2010

I confess of all my wrongs to her—
all the things I've done while we were separated.

This attempt to clear my conscience
ignites flames strong enough
to burn down everything we built.

You're a piece of shit!
Bang!

You're always going to be a fuck up!
Bang!

Go fucken kill yourself!
Bang!

Grow the fuck up already!
Bang!

Go to school you fucken idiot!
Bang!

You're fucken pathetic!
Bang!

This is why no one loves you!
Bang!

This is why everyone leaves you!
Bang!

You're just like your father!
BANG!

I try to explain that all I want is a fresh start,
that shame and guilt claw their way into my heart,
that I can't keep carrying the weight of these secrets,
that it all happened long ago.

But all she says is "Get out,"
with a cracking voice and a cracking heart.

Value
City Terrace, 2010

The only way to keep you happy
is by signing my name
on the designated space of this check.

We hardly speak.

The only messages I receive from you are
"Hey, the phones are due,"
or "You're still getting our boy tomorrow, right?"
and the rare, drunken
"I fucken hate you. You ruined my life."

Two Steps Back

City Terrace, 2010

I gaze at this page, a drunken reflection,
and wonder why I don't just drive to you now,
why I don't just get up off of my ass,
knock on your door, and spill it all out in front of you
rather than onto pages you will never read.

Why haven't I just told you
how fucken sorry I've been,
how sorry I know I'll always be
if I never show you how sorry I truly am?

You see, before you, I was a drunk.
While I had you, I was a man.
And now that you're gone, I am drunk once more.
You, my love, are the cure to my disease.

It's not hard for me to see why I still love you.
It's hard to live with the burden
that I broke our home, your trust, your heart.

Keep an eye out for future publications by Andres Fernandez!

Heavy Steps (chapbook)

Revelry (a collection of short stories)

Conversations with the Night (2010-2016)

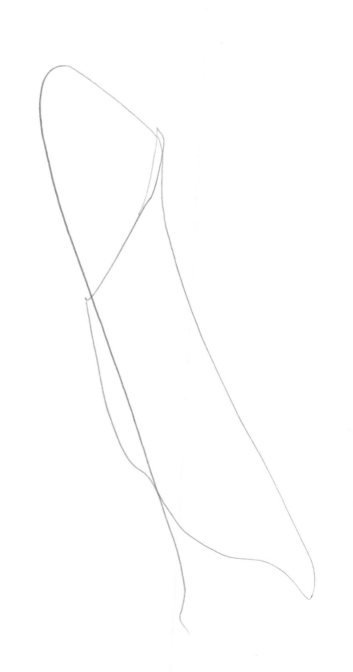

28120381R00101

Printed in Great Britain
by Amazon